Morrells® Handwriting

Letter Formation

Workbook 3

Uses exclusive 'Bounce Technique'

Name ....

Introduction

The Morrells Handwriting workbooks provide a fun and meaningful approach to developing effective handwriting skills. Practice pages teach writing skills, which lay a solid foundation that will last a lifetime.

The workbooks are unique in their method of teaching handwriting and our new workbooks 1 and 2 use our newly developed **'Bounce Technique'**.

The writing activities in this workbook help to reinforce and revise letter formation, placement and spacing in readiness for joined-up handwriting using high-frequency words and grammatical skills.

Neat, legible handwriting quickly becomes routine, allowing the learner to devote all active thinking to the ideas that they are trying to express.

Author: Suzanne Smits
Published by Morrells Handwriting 2014
E-mail: info@morrellshandwriting.co.uk
Web: www.morrellshandwriting.co.uk
Designer: Kate Harber

Suzanne Smits has asserted her right in accordance with the Copyright, Designs and Patents Act, 1988, to be identified as the Author of this work.

All rights reserved. No part of this publication may be reproduced, stored in a retrieval system, copied or transmitted in any way, or by means, electronic, mechanical, photocopying, recording or otherwise without the prior written permission of the Author.

These books are not part of the copyright licensing scheme run by the Copyright Licensing Agency and may not be photocopied or mechanically copied in any other way, without the prior written permission of the Author. The Author prohibits the loaning, photocopying or on selling of this Workbook for purposes of reproduction. Any person found reproducing, copying or transmitting this publication in any way, may be liable to criminal prosecution and civil claims for damages.

Photocopying Prohibited. The copyright in any books, materials and/or products supplied by Morrells Handwriting, or under the Morrells Handwriting brand, belongs solely and exclusively to Morrells Handwriting and may not be altered, reproduced or copied without Morrells Handwriting's written permission. Morrells Handwriting always prosecutes infringement of any copyright.

ISBN: 978-0-9576331-7-9

How to use this workbook

This workbook is the next stage in the development of letter formation that will help embed a fluent writing style and a positive handwriting habit from the beginning. It is important to ensure the writer traces and copies the words correctly into the spaces provided, placing the words correctly on the line. This will automatically correct any problems with writing movement and word spacing, which are all essential for neat handwriting.

Short, but daily practice sessions of 10 minutes are recommended to help improve writing speed.

Key

●   Indicates the starting point of the letter and also the relocation of the pencil (pencil lift)

⟶   Indicates the direction the writer should follow

    Indicates the return direction for the writer to follow (bounce)

123   Numbers indicate the sequence of the letter direction to follow

How you can help

The Morrells Handwriting write-in practice workbooks are designed for children to work through independently.

However, adult supervision is recommended to ensure the following:

- Good sitting position with both feet flat on the floor, knees at 90°, bottom touching the back of the chair, leaning slightly forward and the chair pulled into the desk.
- The correct grip. The dynamic tripod grip with the thumb and the index finger on the pencil. Place the middle finger underneath the pencil with the last two fingers tucked out of the way to help the writer to write for longer without discomfort.
- A relaxed grip for fluent handwriting and to prevent tired hands.
- The writer must trace over all the letters to ensure correct letter shape and direction.
- The paper is tilted in the correct position with both arms on the table.

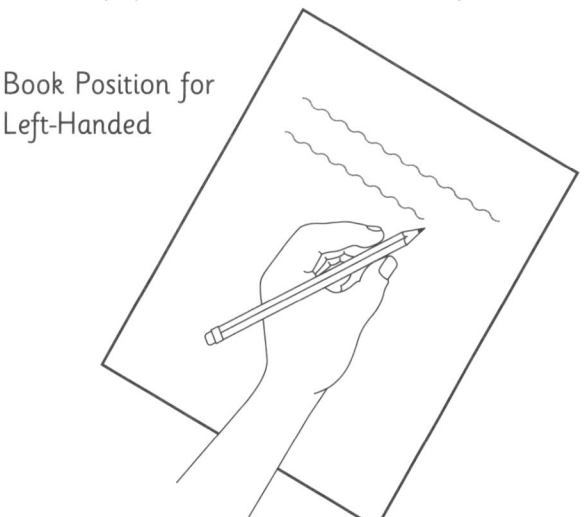

Book Position for Left-Handed

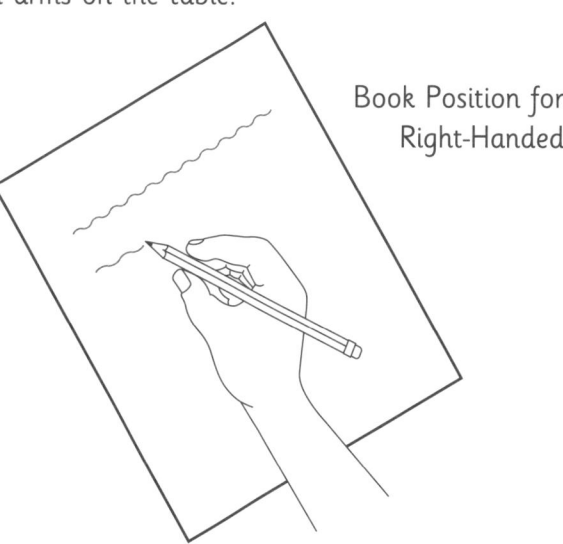

Book Position for Right-Handed

a

High Frequency Words 1
Letters and Sounds

Date _____

Write over the words below.   **Now practise writing the words in the spaces below.**

a   a   a   a

an   an   an   an

as   as   as   as

at   at   at   at

if   if   if   if

in   in   in   in

is   is   is   is

it   it   it   it

of   of   of   of

off   off   off   off

Write over the sentences below.

There was a gigantic snail in my garden.

Mum asked us to turn off the TV.

Now practise writing your own sentence below.

_____

_____

_____

on

High Frequency Words 2
Letters and Sounds

Date

Write over the words below.   Now practise writing the words in the spaces below.

on   on   on   on
can   can   can   can
dad   dad   dad   dad
had   had   had   had
back back   back back
and   and   and   and
get   get   get   get
big   big   big   big
him   him   him   him
his   his   his   his

Write over the sentences below.

The book had fallen noisily to the floor.

You can get more water in this big jug.

Now practise writing your own sentence below.

_____

_____

_____

© Morrells Handwriting. Photocopying prohibited. All rights reserved.   Letter Formation workbook 3

not

High Frequency Words 3
Letters and Sounds

Date

Write over the words below. **Now practise writing the words in the spaces below.**

not   not   not   not
got   got   got   got
up   up   up   up
mum   mum   mum   mum
but   but   but   but
put   put   put   put
the   the   the   the
to   to   to   to
I   I   I   I
no   no   no   no

Write over the sentences below.

I could not get to sleep last night.

Dad put the beautiful picture on the wall.

Now practise writing your own sentence below.

go

**High Frequency Words 4
Letters and Sounds**

Date

Write over the words below.　　Now practise writing the words in the spaces below.

go　　go　　　　　　　　　　　　go　　go
into　into　　　　　　　　　　　into　into
will　will　　　　　　　　　　　will　will
that　that　　　　　　　　　　　that　that
this　this　　　　　　　　　　　this　this
then　then　　　　　　　　　　　then　then
them　them　　　　　　　　　　　them　them
with　with　　　　　　　　　　　with　with
see　see　　　　　　　　　　　　see　see
for　for　　　　　　　　　　　　for　for

Write over the sentences below.

Is this the correct way to the classroom?

I helped to clean the bike with water.

Now practise writing your own sentence below.

Letter Formation workbook 3　　7

now

High Frequency Words 5
Letters and Sounds

Date

Write over the words below.   **Now practise writing the words in the spaces below.**

now   now   now   now
down down   down down
look look   look look
too   too   too   too
he   he   he   he
she   she   she   she
we   we   we   we
me   me   me   me
be   be   be   be
was   was   was   was

Write over the sentences below.

My bath was too hot to jump in.

Tom quickly ran down the steep hill.

Now practise writing your own sentence below.

8   Letter Formation workbook 3   © Morrells Handwriting. Photocopying prohibited. All rights reserved.

you

High Frequency Words 6
Letters and Sounds

Date

Write over the words below.   *Now practise writing the words in the spaces below.*

you   you   you   you
they they   they they
all   all   all   all
are   are   are   are
my   my   my   my
her   her   her   her
went went   went went
it's it's   it's it's
from from   from from
children   children

Write over the sentences below.

The children handed in their homework.

My pet dog went for a walk in the park.

Now practise writing your own sentence below.

just

High Frequency Words 7
Letters and Sounds

Date

Write over the words below.   **Now practise writing the words in the spaces below.**

just   just   just   just
help   help   help   help
said   said   said   said
have   have   have   have
like   like   like   like
so   so   so   so
do   do   do   do
some   some   some   some
come   come   come   come
were   were   were   were

Write over the sentences below.

Cats like to drink milk from a bowl.

There were some socks on the floor.

Now practise writing your own sentence below.

_____

_____

there

High Frequency Words 8
Letters and Sounds

Date

Write over the words below.   **Now practise writing the words in the spaces below.**

there   there   there   there
little   little   little   little
one   one   one   one
when   when   when   when
out   out   out   out
what   what   what   what
don't   don't   don't   don't
old   old   old   old
I'm   I'm   I'm   I'm
by   by   by   by

Write over the sentences below.

There is still one ticket left for sale.

What time are we going to the park?

Now practise writing your own sentence below.

Letter Formation workbook 3

time

High Frequency Words 9
Letters and Sounds

Date

Write over the words below. **Now practise writing the words in the spaces below.**

time time   time time
house house   house house
about about   about about
your your   your your
day day   day day
made made   made made
came came   came came
make make   make make
here here   here here
saw saw   saw saw

Write over the sentences below.

I have made lunch for you today.

Sarah looked at the time on her watch.

Now practise writing your own sentence below.

very

High Frequency Words 10
Letters and Sounds

Date _____

✏️ **Write over the words below.** ✏️ **Now practise writing the words in the spaces below.**

very   very   very   very
oh   oh   oh   oh
their   their   their   their
people people   people people
Mr   Mr   Mr   Mr
Mrs   Mrs   Mrs   Mrs
looked looked   looked looked
called called   called called
asked   asked   asked   asked
could   could   could   could

✏️ **Write over the sentences below.**

Many people like eating bananas.

The brown leaves are very crispy.

✏️ **Now practise writing your own sentence below.**

_____

_____

_____

Verbs

Date _____

✏ Write over the words below.   ✏ Now practise writing the words in the spaces below.

hunt _____ hunt
hunting _____ hunting
hunter _____ hunter
hunted _____ hunted

✏ Write over the words below.   ✏ Now practise writing the words below.

clean
cleaning
cleaner
cleaned

✏ Write over the sentences below.

The blue paint was still wet.
The new painting was a present.
The painter is at work today.
I painted a beautiful picture.

✏ Now practise writing your own sentence below using a verb.

_____

_____

14 Letter Formation workbook 3   © Morrells Handwriting. Photocopying prohibited. All rights reserved.

Verbs

Date

✏️ Write over the words below. ✏️ Now practise writing the words in the spaces below.

help   help
helping   helping
helper   helper
helped   helped

✏️ Write over the words below. ✏️ Now practise writing the words below.

follow
following
follower
followed

✏️ Write over the sentences below.

I can jump through the hoop.
I like jumping into large puddles.
My purple jumper has a hole.
We all jumped into the water.

✏️ Now practise writing your own sentence below using a verb.

Verbs

Date

Write over the words below.   *Now practise writing the words in the spaces below.*

play   play
playing   playing
player   player
played   played

Write over the words below.   *Now practise writing the words below.*

train
training
trainer
trained

Write over the sentences below.

It's a short walk to my house.
We started walking before it rained.
The dog walker is my neighbour.
I walked home instead of taking the bus.

Now practise writing your own sentence below using a verb.

Adverbs

Date _____

✏️ Write over the words below.　　✏️ Now practise writing the words in the spaces below.

happily　　　　　　　　　　　　　　　　　　　happily
quickly　　　　　　　　　　　　　　　　　　　quickly
clearly　　　　　　　　　　　　　　　　　　　clearly
poorly　　　　　　　　　　　　　　　　　　　poorly

✏️ Write over the words below.　　✏️ Now practise writing the words below.

slowly
heavily
carefully
quietly

✏️ Write over the sentences below.

Sam walked quickly to catch the bus.
Without warning, it rained heavily.
The snail crept slowly across the path.
Josh carefully wrote the letter.

✏️ Now practise writing your own sentence below using an adverb.

_____

_____

Letter Formation workbook 3

Adverbs

Date _____

Write over the words below.   **Now practise writing the words in the spaces below.**

easily   easily
luckily   luckily
sleepily   sleepily
safely   safely

Write over the words below.   **Now practise writing the words below.**

thankfully
gently
proudly
plainly

Write over the sentences below.

I washed the thin glasses carefully.
Hannah gracefully danced to the music.
Luckily, the baby slept peacefully.
Outside, the wind howled violently.

Now practise writing your own sentence below using an adverb.

Adjectives

Date

Write over the words below. *Now practise writing the words in the spaces below.*

green green
small small
soft soft
wide wide

Write over the words below. *Now practise writing the words below.*

light
sweet
square
smooth

Write over the sentences below.

Isabelle wore a beautiful green dress.
The wide lorry was too big for the road.
My hungry dog quickly ate his food.
Our new cream sofa is very large.

Now practise writing your own sentence below using an adjective.

Adjectives

Date

✏️ Write over the words below.   ✏️ Now practise writing the words in the spaces below.

high   high
cold   cold
foggy   foggy
hungry   hungry

✏️ Write over the words below.   ✏️ Now practise writing the words below.

dark
heavy
delicious
bright

✏️ Write over the sentences below.

The sun is high up in the blue sky.
My pizza was cold, so I sent it back.
It was dark and damp in the forest.
Be careful, the heavy table may fall!

✏️ Now practise writing your own sentence below using an adjective.

Adjectives

Date _____

Write over the words below.   *Now practise writing the words in the spaces below.*

crashing   crashing

hairy   hairy

growling   growling

round   round

Write over the words below.   *Now practise writing the words below.*

lovely

brave

young

eight

Write over the sentences below.

The young boy ate very slowly.
Tom's eight fish quickly swam away.
I saw the waves crashing on the rocks.
The fresh strawberries are delicious.

Now practise writing your own sentence below using an adjective.

Adjectives

Date _____

✏️ **Write over the sentences below and highlight the adjectives.**

The old man caught a bad cold.

The wooden shed needed painting.

Mum burnt my toast this morning.

Yesterday, was a wet and foggy day.

James was the tallest in our class.

The smaller boy was the loudest.

We met several boys who went fishing.

✏️ **Now practise writing your own sentence below using an adjective.**

Contractions

Date _____

✏️ Write over the words below.   ✏️ Now practise writing the words in the spaces below.

I've _____ I've
I have _____ I have
didn't _____ didn't
did not _____ did not

✏️ Write over the words below.   ✏️ Now practise writing the words below.

I'd _____
I would _____
hasn't _____
has not _____

✏️ Write over the sentences below.

I've not finished my homework yet.
I have not finished my homework yet.
I didn't eat all of my lunch today.
I did not eat all of my lunch today.

✏️ Now practise writing your own sentence below using a contraction.

_____

_____

Contractions

Date

✏️ Write over the words below.   ✏️ Now practise writing the words in the spaces below.

let's let's

let us let us

we're we're

we are we are

✏️ Write over the words below.   ✏️ Now practise writing the words below.

you're

you are

they've

they have

✏️ Write over the sentences below.

Dad's car wasn't ready at the garage.
Let's take out our pencils and pens.
They've already picked up their tickets.
You're too late for dinner!

✏️ Now practise writing your own sentence below using a contraction.

24 Letter Formation workbook 3

Contractions

Date _____

Write over the words below.   Now practise writing the words in the spaces below.

who's   who's
who is   who is
where's   where's
where is   where is

Write over the words below.   Now practise writing the words below.

they'll
they will
that's
that has

Write over the sentences below.

Call me when you've finished eating.
Who's going swimming tomorrow?
They'll get very wet in this heavy rain.
That's got stuck in the large tree.

Now practise writing your own sentence below using a contraction.

_____

_____

Contractions

To Show Possession

Date

✏️ Write over the sentences below.

Sophie's room was pink.
The room belonging to Sophie was pink.

The boys' go-karts are very fast.
The go-karts belonging to the boys are very fast.

The teachers' cars are parked in the large car park at the back of the school.

The cars belonging to the teachers are parked in the large car park at the back of the school.

✏️ Now write your own sentence below using a contraction to show possession.

Conjunctions

Date _____

Write over the words below.   **Now practise writing the words in the spaces below.**

and   and
for   for
whereas   whereas
since   since

Write over the words below.   **Now practise writing the words below.**

until
when
if
while

Write over the sentences below.

I will play football, if I'm on the team.
He saw me, while I waited for the train.
He worked hard, whereas I did very little.
I will wait here until the bus arrives.

Now write your own sentence below using a conjunction.

Conjunctions

Date _____

✏️ Write over the words below. ✏️ Now practise writing the words in the spaces below.

because _____ because _____
which _____ which _____
but _____ but _____
so _____ so _____

✏️ Write over the words below. ✏️ Now practise writing the words below.

therefore _____
next _____
before _____
after _____

✏️ Write over the sentences below.

I like chicken because it's delicious.
Mia tried the soup, but didn't like it.
I could go to the park, or to the beach.
The sun is warm, yet the wind is cold.

✏️ Now write your own sentence below using a conjunction.

_____

_____

Antonyms

Date

✏️ **Write over the words below.** ✏️ **Now practise writing the words in the spaces below.**

happy　　　　　　　　　　　　　　　happy
sad　　　　　　　　　　　　　　　　sad
light　　　　　　　　　　　　　　　light
dark　　　　　　　　　　　　　　　dark

✏️ **Write over the words below.** ✏️ **Now practise writing the antonyms.**

open   close
start   stop
sweet   sour
laugh   cry

✏️ **Write over the sentences and highlight the antonyms.**

During winter the weather is cold, but in the summer it can be very hot.

✏️ **Now practise writing the sentence below.**

Antonyms

Date

✏️ Write over the words below.   ✏️ Now practise writing the words in the spaces below.

full   full
empty   empty
loud   loud
quiet   quiet

✏️ Write over the words below.   ✏️ Now practise writing the antonyms.

push   pull
inside   outside
soft   hard
large   small

✏️ Write over the sentences below and highlight the antonyms.

It was very hot outside.
A cold wind blew into the empty room.
I would like a new bike for my birthday.
The old shed was falling down.

✏️ Now write a list of as many antonyms as you can.

Homophones
Date

✏️ *Write over the words below.* ✏️ *Now practise writing the words in the spaces below.*

brake   break
great   grate
wait   weight
sun   son
herd   heard
aloud   allowed
past   passed
new   knew
write   right
there   their

✏️ *Write over the sentences below and highlight the homophones.*

Mum had to wait for the nurse to check her weight.

✏️ *Now practise writing your own sentence below.*

Homophones

Date _____

✏️ **Write over the sentences below and highlight the homophones.**

You must be quiet when you go inside.
Chantal was stung on her leg by a bee.

The wind blew the kite into the trees.
My new blue pencil is very sharp.

The large herd of cows were in the field.
Oliver heard footsteps behind him.

The two girls bought some fruit. However,
they did not have enough money to buy
a drink as it was too expensive.

✏️ **Now practise writing your own sentences below.**

Speech Marks

Date _____

✏️ **Write over the sentences below.**

"It's time for bed now," said Mum.
Mum said, "It's time for bed now."

"I have new shoes," said Ben.
Ben said, "I have new shoes."

"Follow me to the park," said Nathan.
Nathan said, "Follow me to the park."

"I like fruit for my lunch," said Luke.
Luke said, "I like fruit for my lunch."

✏️ **Now practise writing your own sentences below.**

_____

_____

_____

_____

Speech Marks

✏️ Write over the sentence below.

"I think I know the answer," said Beth.

✏️ Now rewrite the sentence below.

✏️ Write over the sentence below.

Joe said, "I feel worn out today."

✏️ Now rewrite the sentence below.

✏️ Write over the sentence below.

"Please learn your spellings," said Mum

✏️ Now rewrite the sentence below.

✏️ Write over the sentences below.

"It's time for bed," said Mum, "So don't forget to brush your teeth."

"Oh no!" Meg said, "Where have I left my Maths homework?"

Speech Marks

Date _____

✏️ Write over the sentences below.

Charlie shouted, "Watch out!"
"Watch out!" shouted Charlie.

"That's not fair Mum!" cried Beth.
Beth cried, "That's not fair Mum!"

Ellie asked, "What time do we leave?"
"What time do we leave?" asked Ellie.

"It's a beautiful day," said Chantal, "Do you want a chocolate ice-cream from the shop?"

✏️ Now practise writing your own sentences below.

Morrells

Use Morrells Handwriting to follow the new National Curriculum 2014: Handwriting

- ✓ Learn how to hold and use a pencil/pen correctly and sit correctly
- ✓ Teach letter formation in the correct handwriting families
- ✓ Practise and revise the correct letter formation frequently and confidently
- ✓ Teach joined-up handwriting using diagonal and horizontal strokes
- ✓ Understand which letters are best left unjoined

A back to basics approach for poor handwriting, these series of handwriting workbooks offer a simple, but effective solution to handwriting problems.

Based on ability rather than age, they are perfect for children, teenagers and adults.

- Uses the Morrells unique 'Bounce Technique'
- Dyspraxia and Dyslexia friendly resources
- Stimulates muscle memory
- Develops hand eye co-ordination and fine motor strength
- Boosts confidence and learning

Letter Formation

Learn to form letters correctly through lots of handwriting practice with letter shapes and spacing. This will help ensure that the correct letter formation and directional movements are achieved right from the start.

Joined-up Handwriting

Create joined-up handwriting that is smooth, legible, fluent and fast. Master the progressive joining technique of the baseline joins before moving on to the more difficult round and top joins.

Published by Morrells Handwriting 2014
E-mail: info@morrellshandwriting.co.uk
Web: www.morrellshandwriting.co.uk

© Morrells Handwriting. All rights reserved.

ISBN: 978-0957633179

RRP £4.95